# The Beauty of Berlin

## FROM THE TIERGARTEN TO THE BERLIN WALL

### A TRAVEL PHOTO ART BOOK

LAINE CUNNINGHAM

The Beauty of Berlin

From the Tiergarten to the Berlin Wall

A Travel Photo Art Book

Published by Sun Dogs Creations
*Changing the World One Book at a Time*
Print ISBN: 9781951389055

Cover Design by Angel Leya
Cover Photo by Gilly on Unsplash

Copyright © 2019 Laine Cunningham

All rights reserved. No part of this book may be reproduced in any form or by any means, electronic, mechanical, digital, photocopying or recording, except for the inclusion in a review, without permission in writing from the publisher.

# THE TRAVEL PHOTO ART SERIES

*Ruins of Rome I & II*
*Along the Via Appia*
*Garden City Garbatella*
*Ancients of Assisi I & II*
*Captivating Capri*
*Milan Cathedral*
*Treasures of Turin*
*Panoramas of Portugal*
*Linger in Lisbon*
*The Splendors of Sintra*
*Spectacles of Stepantsminda*
*Grandeur in the Republic of Georgia*
*Tableaus of Tbilisi*
*Original Old Tbilisi*
*Marvels of Mtskheta*
*Paragons of Prague*
*Hidden Prague*
*The Pillars of the Bohemian Paradise*
*Lidice Lives*
*Terezín and Theresienstadt*
*Flourishes of France*
*Portraits of Paris*
*Notre Dame Cathedral*
*The Beauty of Berlin*

FACE OFF

NAVIGATOR

MP 73

RIFT

WORK IN PROGRESS

SWEET STREET

RELAXED

KEROUAC

INDUSTRIAL

PORT

CONDUCTOR

EDIFICATION

ENCHANTE

APERTURE

FEARLESS

CAUSEWAY

TATTERS

FREE HUGS

FRECKLES

VESUVIUS

WHERE'S WALDO

SNORT

POPOVERS

ODOODEM

MARVIN THE MARTIAN

GATE OF LIFE

STEELED

ALLOTMENT

CLOWN FACE

BLAZE

FRACTURES

FLINT

FOSSILS

FINAL APPROACH

RECESS

FESTIVAL

STYLUS

# ABOUT THE AUTHOR

Laine Cunningham leads readers around the world. *The Family Made of Dust* is set in the Australian Outback, while *Reparation* is a novel of the American Great Plains. Her travel memoir *Woman Alone* appeals to fans of *Wild* and *Eat Pray Love*.

## NOVELS BY LAINE CUNNINGHAM

*The Family Made of Dust*

*Beloved*

*Reparation*

## OTHER BOOKS BY LAINE CUNNINGHAM

*Woman Alone: A Six-Month Journey Through the Australian Outback*

*On the Wallaby Track*

*Seven Sisters: Spiritual Messages from Aboriginal Australia*

*Writing While Female or Black or Gay*

*Ruins of Rome I & II*
*Along the Via Appia*
*Garden City Garbatella*
*Ancients of Assisi I & II*
*Captivating Capri*
*Milan Cathedral*
*Treasures of Turin*
*Panoramas of Portugal*
*Linger in Lisbon*
*The Splendors of Sintra*
*Spectacles of Stepantsminda*
*Grandeur in the Republic of Georgia*
*Tableaus of Tbilisi*
*Original Old Tbilisi*
*Marvels of Mtskheta*
*Paragons of Prague*
*Hidden Prague*
*The Pillars of the Bohemian Paradise*
*Lidice Lives*
*Terezín and Theresienstadt*
*Flourishes of France*
*Portraits of Paris*
*Notre Dame Cathedral*
*The Beauty of Berlin*

*The Zen of Travel*
*The Zen of Gardening*
*Zen in the Stable*
*The Zen of Chocolate*
*The Zen of Dogs*

*The Wisdom of Puppies*
*The Wisdom of Babies*
*The Wisdom of Weddings*

*The Beautiful Book of Questions*
*The Beautiful Book for Dream Seekers*
*The Beautiful Book for Rebels*
*The Beautiful Book for Women*
*The Beautiful Book for Lovers*

www.ingramcontent.com/pod-product-compliance
Lightning Source LLC
Chambersburg PA
CBHW041320110526
44591CB00021B/2853